FABRIC PAINTING
FOR FUN!

By Anne Schreiber

Content Adviser: Sonja Lee, Friends of Fabric Art, Lowell, Massachusetts
Reading Adviser: Frances J. Bonacci, Ed.D, Reading Specialist, Cambridge, Massachusetts

COMPASS POINT BOOKS
MINNEAPOLIS, MINNESOTA

Compass Point Books
3109 West 50th Street, #115
Minneapolis, MN 55410

Visit Compass Point Books on the Internet at www.compasspointbooks.com
or e-mail your request to custserv@compasspointbooks.com

Photographs ©: Photodisc/Getty, front cover (left); Istockphoto, front cover (right), 6-7, 8 (top), 9, 10-11, 12-13, 14-15, 18, 19, 26; Scott B. Rosen, 4, 5, 8 (bottom), 9 (sponge), 16–17, 27, 28-29 (center), 29 (bottom), 30-31; Ginny Eckley, 4-5 (spread), 32–33; Shutterstock, 21, 22, 24, 25, 42 (right and left), 43 (right and left), 44 (right); Jennie Woodcock/Reflections Photography/Corbis, 23; Photodisc, 28 (bottom), 35 (top); Corel, 34, 35 (bottom), 43 (center), 47; AP Wide World Photos, 36-37, 38, 45 (right); Photos.com, 39, 42 (center), 45 (left); Margaret Courteney-Clarke/Corbis, 20, 40-41; Kelly-Mooney/Corbis, 44 (left)Photographs ©: Photodisc/Getty, front cover; Istockphoto, front cover, 6-7, 8-9, 10-11, 12-13, 14-15, 18-19, 26, (bottom) 35,

Editors: Deb Berry and Aubrey Whitten/Bill SMITH STUDIO; and Shelly Lyons
Designer/Page Production: Geron Hoy, Kavita Ramchandran, Sinae Sohn, Marina Terletsky, and Brock Waldron/Bill SMITH STUDIO
Photo Researcher: Jacqueline Lissy Brustein, Scott Rosen, and Allison Smith/Bill SMITH STUDIO
Art Director: Jaime Martens
Creative Director: Keith Griffin
Editorial Director: Carol Jones
Managing Editor: Catherine Neitge

Library of Congress Cataloging-in-Publication Data

Schreiber, Anne.
  Fabric painting for fun! / by Anne Schreiber.
        p. cm. -- (For fun!)
  Includes bibliographical references and index.
  ISBN 0-7565-1690-0 (hard cover)
  1. Textile painting--Juvenile literature. I. Title. II. Series.

 TT851.S37 2006
 746.6--dc22

                         2005030278

Printed in the United States of America.

Table of Contents

The Basics

INTRODUCTION/Fabric Art for Fun 4

FABRIC PAINTS/When Paint Is Not Just Paint 6

FABRIC PAINTING MATERIALS/What You Need to Begin . 8

PAINTING METHODS/Beyond the Brush 10

PREPARING TO PAINT/Ready, Set, Paint! 12

Doing It

USING STENCILS/Ready-Made Designs 14

BLOCK PAINTING AND STAMPING/

Two Is Better Than One. 16

MARBLE EFFECT/Marbled Cream 18

DYE BASICS/Dyeing for Tie-Dye 20

SALT AND ALCOHOL EFFECTS/Splatters and Halos 22

DISCHARGE ART/Bleach Break 24

PROJECT #1/Glowing Banner. 26

PROJECT #2/Patterned Placemats. 28

PROJECT #3/Fun-in-the-Sun Painting 30

PROJECT #4/Funky Faux Batik 32

People, Places, and Fun

NATURAL DYEING/Wear What You Eat 34

FABRIC ART AROUND THE WORLD/Color Your World . . . 36

THE FABRIC ART OF JAPAN/Kimonos to Curtains. 38

THE FABRIC ART OF AFRICA/From Mud to Korhogo. 40

TIMELINE/What Happened When? 42

TRIVIA/Fun Fabric and Dye Facts. 44

• •

QUICK REFERENCE GUIDE/Fabric Painting

Words to Know. 46

GLOSSARY/Other Words to Know 47

WHERE TO LEARN MORE 47

INDEX 48

Note: In this book, there are two kinds of vocabulary words. Fabric painting Words to Know are words specific to fabric painting. They are defined on page 46. Other Words to Know are helpful words that aren't related only to fabric painting. They are defined on page 47.

Fabric Art for Fun

Whether it's the logo of your favorite band, a freehand drawing of planets and stars, or a crazy tie-dye pattern, fabric painting is everywhere. You'll find it on T-shirts, hats, bags, and socks. But do you know that you can make many of these things yourself? You might want to create costumes for your school play, design uniforms for a club you're in, or brighten up your room with painted pillows. No matter what you want to create, fabric painting is easy to learn and filled with endless possibilities. From brush painting to tie-dyeing, from block printing to sun art, you'll never want to wear a plain white T-shirt again!

When Paint Is Not Just Paint

There are two basic types of fabric paint. One is water-based paint. This is the kind you usually brush on. Water-based paint is set on the surface of the fabric. That's why you can feel it sitting on top of the material. Water-based fabric paint is easy to find, safe to use, and fun to apply. It also comes in many beautiful colors. In addition to solid colors, fabric paint can be metallic (gold and silver), fluorescent (glow-in-the-dark), pearlescent (shimmery), and textured (puff paint).

The other type of fabric paint is known as dye. It is different from paint because it becomes part of the material. It is often called fiber-reactive because the chemicals in the dye actually react with the fabric and change it.

Dyes are harder to use than water-based paints, and they're

messier, too. But once they're on, they feel like part of the fabric. They also stay on much longer without losing their color or pattern.

7

Different Types of Paint

- **Water-based Paint:** goes right on the material and is set by heat drying.

- **Fabric Markers:** come in many colors and line sizes. Use them to draw freehand on fabric or to trace a drawing.

- **Fabric Crayons:** are used like regular crayons. The drawing is then transferred onto fabric by applying a hot iron.

- **Puff Paints:** come in squeeze bottles in many colors and puff up when they dry.

- **Dye:** color that chemically reacts with the fabric, permanently changing it.

What You Need to Begin

It's easy to get started on a fabric painting project. Choose the T-shirt or other fabric that you plan to decorate. A natural fabric, like cotton, works best. Then, look at this list to help you get organized and start painting.

- **Fabric Paints or Dyes:** Know what type of paint you're using and what colors.

- **Palette:** You don't have to buy a real artist's palette to hold your paints. You can use a plate, bowl, or cup for thinner paints.

- **Masking Tape:** Tape is great for attaching your fabric to the table or surface you are working on. It also will help cover what you don't want to paint.

- **Brushes:** Remember to choose the right brush for the right material.

- **Sponges and Q-Tips:** Apply paints or dyes with sponges for special effects or with Q-tips for small dabs of color.

- **Water Containers and Paper Towels:** You'll want to have plenty of fresh water to wash out brushes and keep things clean. Paper towels can be used to clean up any messes.

- **Spray Bottles and Squeeze Bottles:** Diluted paint from a spray bottle will provide an interesting effect.

- **Stencils and Block Prints:** For block printing and stencils, cardboard, potatoes, or other things can be carved or cut.

- **Pens and Chalk:** Sketch your design with pens or use chalk with dark fabrics.

- **Old Clothes, Drop Cloths, Newspapers, and Gloves:** Protect your house and yourself when you paint. You should wear rubber gloves when working with dyes.

Beyond the Brush

There are two basic ways to paint fabric: hand painting directly onto the fabric (with a sponge or a brush) or painting with a template or transfer design.

Brushing It On: The easiest way to paint is with fabric brushes. It's always helpful to sketch your drawing on a sheet of paper. You can use this sketch for reference while you paint.

When you're ready to begin, dip the fabric brush into one color of paint in your palette and apply it directly onto the stretched fabric. Simple geometric patterns like circles and spirals look great and are easy to paint.

3 1833 04889 851 1

Wet-on-Wet Fabric Painting: Paint on top of another color before it dries for a wet-on-wet effect. By adding extra water, you will get a watercolor look. Try splattering on watery paint to create fabric splatter art.

Sponge Painting: Apply your paint with a sponge. Pour the paint into a tray or dish and dip the sponge into it. You can even cut sponges into different shapes for sponge stamping.

Using Templates: A template is a pattern that you create in advance. It's the best way to make sure that a design is going to look exactly the way you want. After cutting out a cardboard template, place it on your fabric and trace around it with a fabric marker.

Using Transfers: Transfers are another way to trace your design right onto the fabric. You can buy iron-on transfers or trace over a paper design with chalk on a sheet of paper. Turn the paper face down onto your fabric and rub gently. The chalk outline will appear on your fabric.

Ready, Set, Paint!

You're almost ready to fabric paint. But first you'll need to choose your fabric.

A plain white T-shirt is always a good choice. If a T-shirt isn't your style, you can paint on sheets, towels, pillow cases, hats, or even sneakers. Just about anything that's made of fabric can be painted, although natural fabrics, such as cotton, will hold the paint the best.

Next, you'll need to figure out what you're going to paint. Even if you're drawing a freehand design, you might want to try out several ideas on a piece of paper, just to see how it looks and what colors work best.

Follow these simple steps to fabric painting success:

1. Choose a flat work surface like a table or counter. Protect the space with newspapers or drop cloths.

2. Wash and dry the material you're going to paint.

3. Iron the material. Make sure your fabric is smooth and wrinkle-free for best results. Ask for help from an adult because irons get very hot.

4. Attach the material to your work surface. Use masking tape to secure the fabric edges to the surface. Make sure it's flat and tight.

5. Separate the back and front of the material by placing newspaper or cardboard between them so the paint doesn't soak through to the back of your fabric.

You are now ready to let the fabric painting fun begin!

Ready-Made Designs

Stenciling is the technique of cutting out a shape that you fill in with paint. Stencils can provide a pattern that repeats over and over again.

You can purchase stencils, or better yet, make your own. To make a stencil, you'll need to create a template with cardboard or foam. Then, ask an adult to help you poke a hole into the middle of your template. Starting at this hole, cut around the template until the shape is cut out. Leave enough of a border to keep the stencil in shape.

Now tape your stencil where you want it to go and dab on your paint with a sponge. When your paint is on, lift up your stencil.

If you are unable to make your own stencil, you can purchase ready-made ones at your local craft store.

Two Is Better Than One

What's better than French fried potatoes? Potatoes turned into block prints! Block printing, or stamping, is when paint is applied to one object, such as a carved potato, and then stamped onto the fabric.

Stamps can be bought in stores, but it's also easy and fun to make your own. In addition to creating potato stamps, you can block print with many other materials.

Sponges also make great stamps. Cut sponge pieces into shapes and dip them in paint. Make sure that the sponge is covered. As with potatoes, you can always apply your paint to the sponge with a paintbrush for less mess.

Nature is a wonderful place to find shapes that will make great stamps. Leaves, flowers, and shells can be used as fabric stamps. Also try using common objects such as coins, buttons, and curly uncooked pasta for unusual designs.

Marbled Cream

Marbling is a technique that creates an incredible swirl of patterns that resembles marble. Legend has it that marbling was invented in the 12th century when a member of the Japanese royal family accidentally dropped ink in water. He noticed that the ink floated to the surface. When he put a piece of paper on top of the floating ink, marbling was invented.

Modern day marbling is a little more difficult than it was nine centuries ago. Here is a simple way to enjoy the beauty of marbling:

Supplies

white shaving cream and dye

- Spray the shaving cream into a long flat tray.

- Next, squeeze different colors of fabric dye on top of the cream.

- Then, using a chopstick, a spoon, or most commonly, a comb, stir through the paint and a marbled design occurs.

- Once the design is created, lay the fabric on top and it will soak up the pattern. After it dries, the marbled fabric is ready to show off.

Dyeing for Tie-Dye

How does dyeing compare to painting? Dyes stay on longer, have vibrant colors, and blend smoothly with fabric. But working with dyes can be tricky. The most popular dyeing technique is tie-dyeing.

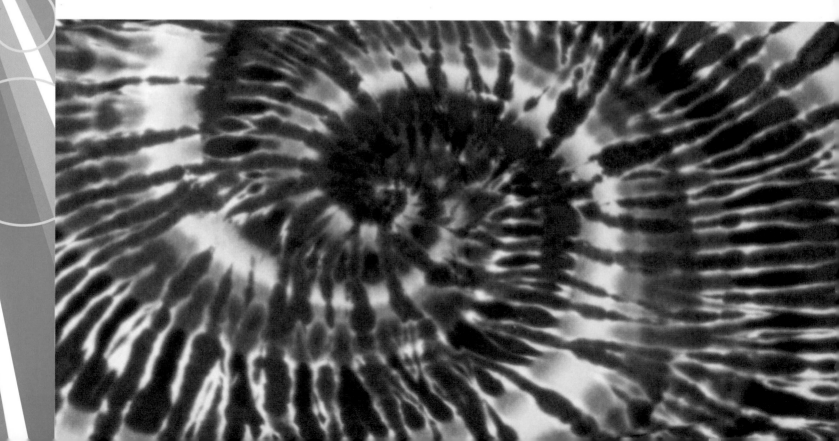

Dyes are chemicals, and you have to be careful when you handle them. When you tie-dye, always wear gloves; if you are dyeing indoors, you should wear a mask around your nose and mouth so you don't inhale the fumes. Using natural dyes, or dyes that you make yourself, makes tie-dyeing less dangerous, is better for the environment, is fun to experiment with, and makes great colors.

Tie-dye tints can be purchased at a craft store or grocery store, and all come with directions for their use. Tie-dyeing looks best with natural fibers, so use cotton, silk, or other natural materials.

Strange Moments In Dyeing

You might think tie-dyeing was invented by hippies in the 1960s. In fact, tie-dyeing is an ancient fabric art dating back to 2500 B.C. Scientists have found tie-dyed cloth in the tombs of Egyptian mummies. Now, the colorful look of tie-dye is once again in style.

Splatters and Halos

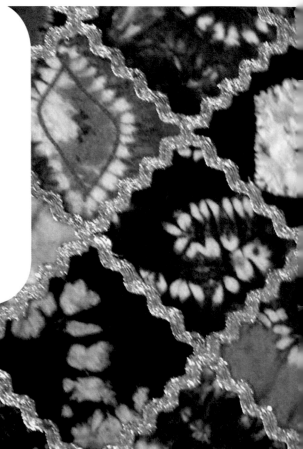

Now that you know the painting basics, you're ready to move on to special effects.

Salt and rubbing alcohol are two substances you can use to create unusual shapes and patterns. Both effects work best when you're using the wet-on-wet method.

To create salt effects, sprinkle salt over the fabric while the fabric paint is still wet. The salt will begin to absorb the paint that it is touching, leaving certain areas of the fabric with less paint. When the fabric is dry, simply brush off the salt.

For alcohol painting, make sure the painted fabric is damp but not soaking wet. Then, using a paintbrush or a cotton swab, drop on a small amount of rubbing alcohol. Wherever the alcohol lands, it will push the paint away, causing a pattern of rings and halos.

Bleach Break

Have you ever accidentally spilled bleach on your shirt? Where the bleach spilled, the fabric turned white.

In discharge dyeing, the color is removed on purpose. Discharge dyeing means to discharge, or remove, the original color from the fabric. The best thing to do this with, of course, is bleach.

Bleach, which is diluted with water, can be applied in a number of different ways—a spray bottle, an eye dropper, a paint brush, or a block print. It can even be splattered on. Where the bleach goes, the color disappears, leaving an interesting pattern behind.

The bleach should stay on the fabric for about five minutes. But as soon as the bleach has soaked in, the fabric has to be rinsed in something that will stop the bleach from eating away at the fabric. A vinegar and water mixture will work.

Glowing Banner

This banner does more than just hang; you can make it glow-in-the-dark. Follow these instructions and you'll have a cool banner to hang in your room or outside your house.

What You Need

- Black paper
- White chalk
- Colored chalk
- Fluorescent paints
- Masking tape
- A thin dowel (a little wider than your fabric)
- Black or darkly colored fabric (a rectangular piece)
- Newspaper
- Fabric glue
- Squeeze bottles or brushes

What you do:

1. Tape your black or dark fabric to a clean, flat surface. Leave 3 inches (8 cm) of the material on the right side for your hanging stick.

2. Draw your design on a black piece of paper using colored chalk. Then copy your design, by hand, on your fabric using white chalk.

3. Go over your chalk outlines with fluorescent paints.

4. Let the paint dry.

5. Turn the fabric over. Place one dowel (or stick) across the top of the fabric. Roll the top of the fabric over the dowel and glue it.

6. Put your banner in a light source or in sunlight for at least 20 minutes. Then turn off the lights and watch your artwork glow!

Patterned Placemats

You can make a basic potato or sponge print shape and create a complex pattern by repeatedly stamping the simple shape. By dipping your shape into different colors, you can create a beautiful pattern.

What You Need

- Rectangle of fabric
- Precision knife
- Fabric paints
- Potatoes and sponges
- Tape
- Paper towels
- Tray or dish for colors
- Pens or markers

What You Do:

1. Lay your fabric on a flat surface and tape it down.

2. Cut a potato in half. Draw your shape onto the potato or sponge with a pen or marker. Simple shapes like diamonds and crescents work best.

3. Carve your stamp by cutting away parts of the potato or sponge around your drawing.

4. If using potatoes, dry them gently with a paper towel. Sponges should be slightly damp.

5. Dip the potato, print side down, into a dish of paint.

6. Start in the middle of your fabric. Press the shape firmly onto your cloth. Then press down again, with the same shape, next to your first image. Continue.

7. Completely cover the fabric, using the same shape but different colors, to add interest.

8. When the paint is dry, your placemat is complete.

Fun-in-the-Sun Painting

Sun painting is a great way to combine natural and manufactured objects into an incredible piece of art. It is a wet-on-wet technique. It works by placing objects on top of a wet fabric painting, then putting all of it into direct sunlight to dry. The uncovered fabric will dry faster and will soak up the remaining paint. The covered parts will then have less paint underneath. When they dry, you can see the shapes on the fabric.

What You Need

- Canvas bag
- Hard surface
- Tape
- Fabric paints
- Paintbrush
- Spray bottle
- Objects from nature
- Plenty of sunshine

What You Do:

1. Lay your canvas bag on a hard surface and tape it into place.

2. Put a layer of cardboard in between the front and back of the bag.

3. Paint one side of the bag with two or three different colors. Add an extra coat of water with the spray bottle.

4. Take the bag out into the sun and lay objects on top.

5. Arrange the objects on the bag before the paint dries.

6. Let the bag sit in direct sunlight for 15 minutes to an hour until the paint dries.

7. Remove the objects.

8. Repeat with the other side of the bag.

9. When both sides are finished, set the design by ironing for two to three minutes.

Ideas for Sun Painting Shapes:
- shells
- feathers
- pine cones
- leaves
- paper dolls
- paper snowflakes
- buttons
- forks

Funky Faux Batik

Batik is a form of "resist" painting that has been practiced for centuries. For any kind of resist art, wax or gutta (a rubberlike substance) is painted onto fabric. Then the fabric is dunked into a dye bath. Any areas covered by the wax or gutta will resist the dye or paint. The result is a beautiful crackled look.

Real batik involves working with hot wax and then boiling off the wax after the fabric is painted. This can be very messy! But there are "faux" (fake) batik methods that are neater, easier, and result in the same look.

What You Need

- White cotton T-shirt
- Water-based resist (available at most craft stores)
- Paintbrushes
- Cardboard
- Fabric paints or dyes
- Gutta applicators

1. Lay your T-shirt on a flat surface with a piece of cardboard between the front and back layers of the shirt.

2. Paint on your design using a water-based resist. You can apply the resist with gutta applicators, paintbrushes, stencils, or even rubber stamps.

3. When the resist is dry, paint the T-shirt using different colors of fabric paints or dyes.

4. Allow 24 hours for the paint to dry.

5. Once the shirt is completely dry, heat set the paint with an iron.

6. Hand wash your shirt in warm water with a mild soap to remove the resist.

Faux Batik looks different everytime you do it. It can look very much like tie-dye. Try this project to see what you get.

33

Wear What You Eat

Natural dyes come from plants or rocks. Sometimes, you use the bark, the flower, the berries, the seeds, or the leaves of a plant to create a dye.

To make the dye, plant material is chopped into small pieces and placed in a pot. Water is added and the mixture is usually cooked for several hours or even days. Sometimes the plant matter is pounded into a powder or paste before it is mixed with water. This dye stew can take a long time to gain rich color, but it will look great when it's ready.

Natural Dyes

cochineal–whole dried insects; colors: fuchsia, purple

henna–tree leaves from Egypt; colors: yellow, brown

indigo–whole plant; color: blue

madder root–plant root; colors: pink, red

marigold–dried flower heads; colors: yellow, orange

pomegranate–rinds from a tropical fruit; colors: red, yellow, green

Color Your World

Fabric painting and dyeing have been practiced in all parts of the world. A look around the globe will show the designs that have come from different places. Often, the plants and stones of a certain area will lead the people there to design things with certain colors. Cultural beliefs will lead to different design ideas.

The Shipibo Indians live along the Amazon River in Peru. Their fabrics show the story of their lives in the Amazon forest. The patterns they draw often show the giant anaconda, a snake that lives near them, or the constellations that light up the night sky.

The art of batik is everywhere in Indonesia, especially on the island of Java. Traditional colors in Java are beige, brown, blue, and black, and they are usually made from natural ingredients. The rich blue of batik

art is made from mixing the leaves of the indigo plant with molasses, sugar, and lime. Many people also thought the batik designs had mystical powers that could bring good fortune or keep away bad luck.

India was originally known for its vegetable dye techniques and has produced fabrics with bright and beautiful colors. In Rajastan, handwoven cotton is printed with a red dye, and then mud is layered on top as a resist. When the mud dries, the whole cloth is soaked in an indigo dye bath. The parts covered with mud are red, and the rest of the cloth is blue.

Around the World

Everywhere you go, people around the world are practicing both traditional and new forms of fabric art.

Kimonos to Curtains

Some of the most incredible kinds of fabric art started in Japan. Japanese artists use a type of paste resist, like the wax resist of batik, to create patterns.

One style is freehand drawing of the paste resist. In this method, known as *tsutsugaki*, a squeeze cone is made and rice paste is put inside and squeezed out onto the cloth. The material is then dipped in a dye bath. The rice paste resists the dye, so the dye only goes where there was no paste.

Another style uses stenciling, or *katazome*. Stencils are made by gluing together three sheets of handmade mulberry paper with persimmon glue. Designs are cut from the glued paper. Rice paste resist is applied inside the stencils, the stencils are removed, and the cloth is dyed.

The ancient art form known as *shibori* is very similar to tie-dye. The method involves tying parts of the cloth so that dye won't go to those areas. There are many different ways that this is done, from stitching and winding to folding and clamping.

From Mud to *Korhogo*

Mali

Ivory Coast

The elegant style of African fabrics is well known, with different styles and designs coming from different parts of the continent.

Mud cloth is a handmade cloth from Mali, a country in West Africa. The patterns in mud cloths symbolize different things. Some are abstract images of cowrie shells or grasshoppers.

Korhogo cloth comes from Ivory Coast. The cloth was traditionally made to protect the Senufo people from the spirits they believed were living around them. The cloth is decorated with simple figures of humans, stars, birds, snakes, fish, and lions.

Mud cloth is dyed with mud and other vegetable dyes.

What Happened When?

| 3000 B.C. | 2600 | 300 | 200 | 200 A.D. | 400 |

3000 Printing blocks are used.

2600 Earliest written record for the use of dye in China is registered.

327 Alexander the Great finds fabrics painted in all colors on a trip to India.

200 Early examples of resist techniques are used in Peru.

200 Block printing is invented in China. The Chinese introduce resist and stencils to Japan.

300 Papyrus that contains a dye recipe is placed in a grave. It is the oldest known dye recipe today.

400 Batik is developed in Java, Indonesia.

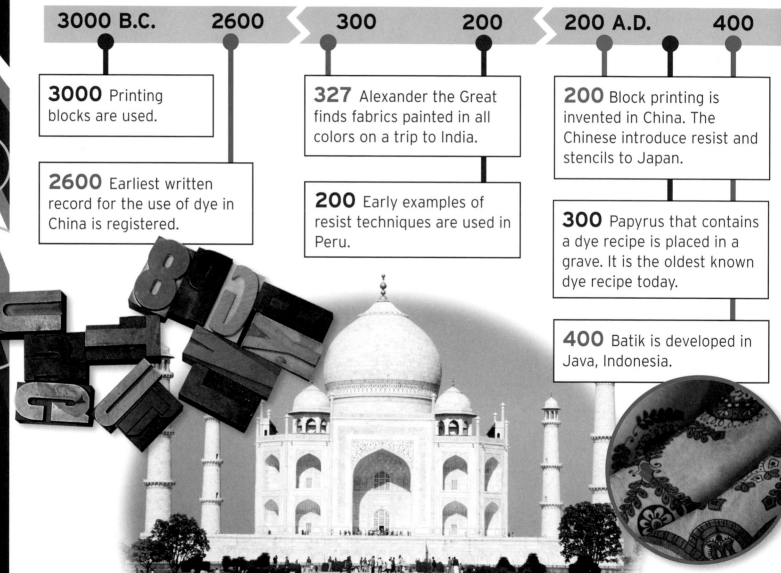

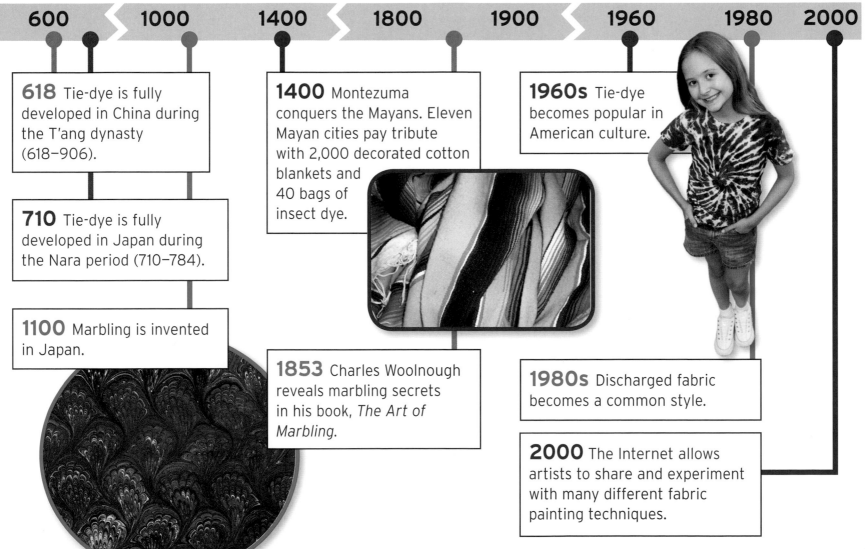

600   **1000**   **1400**   **1800**   **1900**   **1960**   **1980**   **2000**

618 Tie-dye is fully developed in China during the T'ang dynasty (618–906).

710 Tie-dye is fully developed in Japan during the Nara period (710–784).

1100 Marbling is invented in Japan.

1400 Montezuma conquers the Mayans. Eleven Mayan cities pay tribute with 2,000 decorated cotton blankets and 40 bags of insect dye.

1853 Charles Woolnough reveals marbling secrets in his book, *The Art of Marbling.*

1960s Tie-dye becomes popular in American culture.

1980s Discharged fabric becomes a common style.

2000 The Internet allows artists to share and experiment with many different fabric painting techniques.

Fun Fabric and Dye Facts

During the American Revolution, the British soldiers, known as red coats, dyed their coats red with madder root.

In 273, the Roman Emperor Aurelian wouldn't let his wife buy a silk dress dyed with a purple dye known as purpura. His reason was that the dress actually cost its weight in gold!

In ancient Japan, warlords gave gifts to soldiers who showed great bravery. The most prized of all gifts was a tie-dyed kimono.

During the Great Depression of the 1930s, people cut up flour sacks, tie-dyed them, and made them into clothing, curtains, and tablecloths.

In the 15th century, the Turks printed important documents on marbled paper. Because every marbled design is unique, these documents could not be forged or copied.

The earliest samples of cloth dyed with the red dye madder root were buried in King Tutankhamen's tomb around 1339 B.C.

In the old days, areas of cloth were tied and then dyed in a process known as *bandhani,* which means "tie." That's where the English word "bandana" comes from.

In the late fourth century, Emperor Theodosium of the Byzantium Empire forbid his citizens to wear clothing dyed certain shades of purple. The penalty for breaking this rule was death! The shades of purple were only to be worn by members of the royal family.

45

Fabric Painting Words to Know

batik: a form of wax resist

block prints: prints made with paint placed on a stamp and then on the fabric

discharge art: a way of taking the dye out of a fabric with bleach

fabric: the material you paint on

fluorescent: glow-in-the-dark paint

gutta: a rubber-based resist

marbling: a way to float paint on a watery gel or cream and place fabric on top

mud cloth: a traditional dyeing method from Africa

natural dyes: dyes made from plants or minerals

natural materials: cotton, silk, hemp, or other fabrics made of plant fibers

pearlescent: paint that shimmers

puff paint: textured paint that puffs up when it dries

resist: a substance, like wax, that is placed on the fabric that resists, or repels, dye

salt effects: a style of pouring paints on wet fabric and adding salt for special designs

shibori: an ancient form of tie-dye from Japan

sponge painting: using a sponge to apply the paint

stamping: block printing

stencil: a pre-cut shape that is filled in with paint

sun painting: a way to put objects on wet paint and dry them in the sun to create a pattern

template: a pattern you apply paint in to get an exact shape

tie-dye: way of dyeing fabric by tying the fabric and dipping it in dye

transfers: a way to take your design from one place (like paper) to another (like a shirt)

water-based paint: fabric paints that you brush on and that stay on the surface of the material

wet-on-wet: style of painting a second color while the first color is still wet

GLOSSARY

Other Words to Know

abstract: an image of something that is changed from how it really looks

complicated: having many parts

geometric: simple shapes, like squares and rectangles, used in design and decoration

kimono: a long robe with big sleeves, worn by people in Japan

palette: a tray for holding paints

special effects: unusual visual images or patterns

technique: skills, form, and physical movements needed for an activity

traditional: relating to customs that are handed down from one generation to the next

unique: one of a kind, unlike any other

Where To Learn More

AT THE LIBRARY

Luke-Boone, Ronke. *African Fabrics*. Iola, Wis.: Krause Publications, 2001.

Morgenthal, Deborah. *The Ultimate T-Shirt Book*. Asheville, N.C.: Lark Books, 1998.

Innes, Miranda. *Fabric Painting*. New York: Collins & Brown Limited, 1996.

ON THE ROAD

The Fabric Workshop and Museum
1315 Cherry St., 5th floor
Philadelphia, PA 19107
215/568-1111

ON THE WEB

For more information on FABRIC PAINTING use FactHound to track down Web sites related to this book.

1. Go to www.facthound.com
2. Type in this book ID: 0756516900
3. Click on the *Fetch It* button.

Your trusty FactHound will fetch the best Web sites for you!

INDEX

Alcohol painting, 22-23

Bandhani, 45
Batik, 32-33, 36
Bleaching, 24-25
Block printing (stamping),
  16-17
Brushing, 10

Dyes, 6-8, 20-21

Fabric paints, markers,
  crayons, and dyes, 6-8
Fluorescent painting, 6,
  26-27

Katazome, 39
Korhogo, 40

Marbling, 18-19
Masking tape, 8, 13
Mud cloth, 40

Natural dyeing, 34-35

Pearlescent painting, 6
Puff paint, 6-7

Resist, 32-33

Salting, 22-23

Senufo Indians, 40-41
Shibori, 39
Shipibo Indians, 36
Sponging, 11
Stencils, 14
Sun painting, 30-31
Supplies, 8-9, 30, 32

Templates, 11
Tie-dyeing, 20-21
Transfers, 11
Tsutsugaki, 38

Wet-on-wet, 11
Woolnough, Charles, 43

ABOUT THE AUTHOR

Anne Schreiber develops educational materials for kids and teachers. She has created videos, school products, computer games, and lots of fiction and nonfiction books. On weekends, you can find her in her backyard in Brooklyn, tie dyeing!